MONUMENTAL GHOSTS

MONUMENTAL GHOSTS

Alice Bullock

Sunstone Press
Santa Fe, New Mexico

Copyright © 1987 by the estate of Alice Bullock
All Rights Reserved.
No part of this book may be reproduced in any form or by any electronic
or mechanical means including information storage and retrieval systems,
without permission in writing from the publisher,
except by a reviewer who may quote brief passages in a review.

First Edition

Printed in the United States of America

Library of Congress Cataloging in Publication Data:

Bullock, Alice, 1904-1986
   Monumental ghosts.

   1. Monuments--New Mexico--Folklore. 2. Legends--
New Mexico. 3. National parks and reserves--
New Mexico--Folklore. I. Title.
GR110.N6B82   1986   398.2'09789   85-8164
ISBN: 0-86534-029-3

Published in 1987 by SUNSTONE PRESS
        Post Office Box 2321
        Santa Fe, NM 87504-2321 / USA

CONTENTS

- PREFACE 6
- INTRODUCTION 7
1. VIETNAM CHAPEL
   in the Moreno Valley near Eagle Nest 9
2. DORSEY MANSION
   near Springer but off the highway to Clayton 13
3. FORT UNION
   near Watrous 18
4. TSANKAWI,
   part of Bandelier but near White Rock 22
5. CORONADO STATE MONUMENT
   near Bernalillo 25
6. QUARAI,
   now a part of Salinas National Monument,
   near the Town of Mountainair 28
7. LINCOLN TOWN 34
8. CITY OF ROCKS
   near Silver City 37
9. WHITE SANDS
   at Alamogordo 39
10. THE BRIDAL COUPLE,
    White Sands National Park 42

PREFACE

Alice Bullock, a well known author and "doer" moved to Santa Fe in 1941 from Colfax County, New Mexico, where she had grown up and taught in country schools.

She never lost her love for the scattered villages in the country-side, where she learned much of the history of the early settlers and their folklore while helping her husband, Dale Bullock, who was in the newspaper field.

This combination of talents in writing and education together with her voracious reading and uncanny extra-sensory perception made her a special person.

Alice Bullock gained a reputation for her well-written reviews on books which she received from publishers throughout the country.

On assignment from a local newspaper, she wrote many articles on small towns and remote villages and the people who lived in them. In this way she learned of the history and folklore of these villages. She took up photography and recorded many isolated areas and their people.

With her camera and her notebook and her talent for story telling she demonstrated her natural empathy for the people who told the stories she shared with us. Hence, *Monumental Ghosts* is a legacy to her friends, proselytes, and to the **ALICE BULLOCK FAN CLUB**.

Other books still available are: *Mountain Villages, Squaw Tree, Loretto, Discover Santa Fe,* and *Living Legends.*

Loraine Lavender

INTRODUCTION

Do you believe in ghosts?

The objective type personality may well answer, "Of course not! That's all a crock of superstitious twaddle!" The subjective type personality may answer, "I don't know. I haven't seen the pyramids or the Taj Mahal, but a lot of people have, and I believe them when they tell me what they've seen."

Of course, with this type of thing, pictures can be taken or paintings made, while with ghosts, it is at least questionable.

What bothers me the most, I think, is that people of all races, colors, or religions all over the world speak of ghosts they have seen or experienced. I can't feel that all these people have been deceived or are too imaginative or foolish. I believe in the great Chinese Wall. Why shouldn't I believe in the heart-broken mother who saw her son die on a battlefield a continent away?

Once in awhile the belief in a ghost question has a real stopper of an answer, "I didn't, until I had an experience with one," an individual will say.

Now, I know there are ghosts and I don't want to argue about them. I don't care, really, what you believe. I know. For those who like ghost stories, belief is not necessary for enjoyment. They are fun and the darker the night, the more fun they are.

The ghosts in this volume are all "residents" of national or state monuments. Our ghosts in New Mexico, unlike those of say, the British Isles, are rarely vicious or frightening. They are gentle ghosts and more afraid of us, apparently, than we are of them. Let me conclude with the world's shortest ghost story: "The last man on earth sat down in his room. Suddenly, there was a resounding knock on the door!"

THE VIETNAM MEMORIAL CHAPEL

On Memorial Day, May 30, 1983, the Chapel Victor Westphall erected to honor his son, David, and overlooking Eagle Nest Lake in northern New Mexico, became a National Shrine under auspices of the Disabled American Veterans.

Dr. and Mrs. Westphall, and their two sons, lived on a ranch well up on the slopes of Moreno Valley, about half-way from Eagle Nest to where the highway begins to climb over the mountains to Taos.

David, the elder son, whistled for his faithful dog and went for a walk down toward the Eagle Nest Lake. He had enlisted for service in Vietnam and tomorrow he would leave.

David had packed all of his boyhood books in cartons for the Eagle Nest school. One book he could not part with was about eagles which told him about different species and their habitats. He loved it as he loved eagles.

He stopped on the brow of a gently rolling hill below the isolated farm house here in this historic and rich valley. To the north was majestic old Mt. Baldy, reflected and distorted by wind ripples in the lake. The reflection of white thunderheads rolling lazily toward Angel Fire ski run showed at the lower end of the lake. Then he turned slowly to photograph in his memory once again the towering Mt. Wheeler, highest peak in New Mexico. At his back, a cotton-tail zig-zagged across the tall-growing gramma grass. David's dog yipped happily and darted off, only to be recalled by his master's whistle. Obediently he trotted back, tongue dripping, tail wagging, to nip playfully at his heels on the way back to the ranch house.

David's father had watched his son's walk, knowing that the boy had wanted to be alone. From the kitchen came the odors of David's favorite foods. His mother was fixing them for this last supper at home before leaving for service overseas.

It was fate that he would not come back for in Vietnam a sniper's bullet inflicted a fatal wound.

The family grieved, as thousands of families have, when the yellow telegram came. Now, it was Victor who whistled for the dog and walked down to the brow of the hill where David had stood saying farewell to the mountains he loved.

The pain wouldn't go away and it didn't help the Westphalls when their only remaining son announced, with white lips, "I'm going to Vietnam, too. I have to." He wouldn't listen to any one but went to stand in his brother's shoes on another continent.

At the ranch in Moreno Valley, Victor agonized and finally made up his mind. He would build a small chapel, where David had stood, and in his honor.

There were times when he wasn't sure of his own sanity. He would hear the faint strains of David's guitar on the night winds. Then he would find the instrument which was on a cord at the head of David's bed, lying carelessly across the bed. There was a slight indentation of the blankets as though someone had sat there picking out the melodies David had loved.

Victor found that he could not work, really, on the historical volume he was researching and writing and instead he began work on the foundation of the chapel — always accompanied by David's dog.

Victor used not only his own savings but David's insurance money to purchase materials for the chapel. A young Santa Fe architect had drawn plans for the chapel and now toiled as a construction worker, though he had no experience in actual building.

The walls of the odd-shaped chapel climbed while funds for the building dwindled. Victor continued to work while David's dog lay close-by his side. Sometimes the dog would wander out back of the chapel, and howl the misery of all dogs who miss their master. Victor would seek him out, rub his ears, and talk to him until the dog wagged his tail and followed him back into the chapel.

Back at the ranch, Mrs. Westphall, a quiet, motherly woman, silently took care of her household chores and tried to stifle her grief. It was hard when she went to the kitchen to stoke the woodstove, and when once in awhile, she would find David's field cap on the kitchen table, just as he used to drop it when returning from a hunt or would toss it carelessly on the table. When snow carpeted the hills, a small patch of melting crystals and puddled muddy water appeared in front of the refrigerator. When he came home he would eat anything left over from a meal, a chunk of cheese, a slice or so of bologna, and in spite of her admonition, sometimes drank directly from the milk carton.

Silently she cleaned up the floor and hung David's cap back on the deerhorn rack in his room. After all she was his mother and he still lived in her heart.

When the family cash was exhausted, the Westphalls sold the ranch. Victor traveled back from their new home in Springer to continue his work of building the chapel.

As he worked, he gradually realized that this could not be for David alone, but for all the boys from the United States who had given their lives in Vietnam. In his mind's eye he envisioned an eternal flame, and perhaps a carillon to ring out over the quiet Moreno Valley as a prayer for peace.

It was a quiet sunshiny day when another shock came. David's dog, who always accompanied Victor to the Valley, had trotted outside as he often did. Victor heard the sharp crack of a rifle and a single agonized yelp from the dog.

Dropping his trowel, he rushed out, only to see the dog gushing blood from a wound in his chest. Quickly, he swept the Valley with his eyes. There was no one anywhere in sight. A few cows grazed placidly just inside the highway fence, but no human being, with or without a rifle.

David's dog had been killed by a sniper, just as David had been. A school bus purred down the highway below and topped a hill a mile away. Silence.

Victor lifted the dying dog's head, and in spite of himself, sobbed. The dog's tail lifted to wag once, then went limp. It was over. Victor sat absently patting the dog's smooth fur for some time then heavily strode to his pickup for a shovel. He would bury the dog here where he had died.

The earth was hard and rocky. Progress was slow. The sun wouldn't wait for him to finish and the grave was not yet deep enough. Reverently he picked up the dog and carried him inside the chapel. He stretched him out on a work bench, pulled off his jacket and covered him. With real grief, he crawled into his pickup to drive back to Springer. He would finish the burial the next morning.

When Victor returned to the chapel the next morning, the grave that he had begun was filled and another dug a short distance away. Standing by it was a wooden coffin just the right size for the dog.

Silently, he brought the dog's body out, placed him in the coffin, and finished the burial. There was nothing to tell Victor who had dug the grave or constructed the coffin.

He wiped his forehead with the sleeve of his jacket and looked up. Circling the towers of the unfinished chapel were two eagles.

THE DORSEY MANSION

There isn't a thing about the old Dorsey Mansion that is ordinary.

Located on the Clayton highway out of Springer, it stands at the foot of a mesa on what was the Cimarron cut-off of the old Santa Fe Trail.

Who expects to see an old-fashioned Mansion that is partly a two-and-a-half story log house plus a medieval rock castle complete with turreted tower, carved faces surmounted by gargoyles, a huge carriage house and a formal lily pond, in the grasslands of cattle country in northern New Mexico? It just doesn't make sense!

Not even the ghosts adhere to normal folklore. The first reported is that of an old "yeller" steer, long-horned variety, with an error in his genetic strain. One horn is crumpled and his left hind foot twisted sideways.

It is necessary to know at least a little about the Dorsey Mansion, now a state-owned Monument and being restored from years of neglect. When you know how, and who built it, you may appreciate it more.

It was originally built by Stephen W. Dorsey, born of immigrant parents in Vermont. He must have had an over-dose of ambition, for when the family moved to Sandusky, Ohio, while he was still quite young, he promptly got a part-time job with an industrial firm. He held on to this job all through his schooling years, including college.

He was a good student and advanced in his job rapidly, particularly after his marriage to the boss' daughter, the gorgeous and beautiful Helen.

After their daughter died in early childhood, the young Dorseys moved to Arkansas where he became involved in railroading and politics. Dorsey was elected to the United States Senate for one term where he became popular with men of power and money. Dorsey, himself, made money but he and his wife spent a lot, too. They were known for statewide dinners and parties.

Dorsey then decided he wanted to become a cattle baron. He had visited New Mexico with political big-wigs and soon selected a spot on the Santa Fe Trail, then known as Chico Springs. Manipulations on the acquisition of the "Una de Gato" land grant are not clear. Whether he pulled strings or was being pulled is not certain.

He built the log part of the Mansion of oiled logs, hardwood floors, and elaborate fireplaces. The lily pool was shaped like an overturned hobby horse, with a large gazebo on one of the islands in a rather large area of the water space.

It all took money and Dorsey used it lavishly. One estimate was that this "spread" cost at least $50,000, and this was in the 1880's.

The Dorseys entertained not only northern New Mexico society but many visitors of importance, particularly from the East. Guests came too far just to have dinner, a dance, and then leave. Additional quarters soon became a necessity.

Stephen sent to Italy for stonemasons and used native rock to build the "castle" addition to the main house. Again, no expense

Residence of Stephen Dorsey, Chico, New Mexico, 1939. Photo courtesy Museum of New Mexico (Neg. No. 14780).

was spared. Parquetry floors, an art gallery-ballroom combination with a mahogany cathedral ceiling was built. The dining room seated fifty guests without crowding.

A green house was built so that Mrs. Dorsey could have flowers for her dinner tables. The yard was planted with trees and flower beds were in formal designs. There were at least three fountains spraying cooling waters on a hot day.

The stone section contains the tower graced with sculptured faces of Stephen, his wife Helen, and his brother. The faces are surrounded with traditional Renaissance gargoyles. The stone addition is entered through a stained glass ornamented door and entrance way. It contains a fabulous cherrywood staircase rising from the parlor and a blood-onyx fireplace. There are kitchens, butler's pantry, bedrooms, 14 rooms at least.

The basement contained the wine cellar, meat lockers and storage space. While this elaborate section of the house was being built, the ghost that still paces the upstairs hall is said to have met his death here.

Workmen, of course, had nothing to do when the day's work had been done. It was too far from any town for them to ride horseback for any recreation. Bored men tend to become short of temper and the Italians and native workmen did not get along well.

While working in putting up the stone walls in the basement, two of the men became angry and fought. One struck the head of the other with a great mallet. Realizing, then, that he had committed murder, the survivor quickly sealed the body behind the stone slabs thus concealing him forever.

It is said that this man is the one to walk the halls though why the upstairs hall is not known. I have heard footsteps in this hall at night but were they those of a ghost? It sounded more like those of a man. It never occurred to me to be frightened!

Mr. and Mrs. K. E. Deaton, from Texas, had bought the dilapidated mansion in 1966 and had set out to restore it to its original grandeur. Later they yielded to the State of New Mexico which decided it was worthy of preservation and restoration as a State Monument.

The Deatons were unable to sleep their first night and set up camp beds in the dining room because of the incessant pacing. They explored the house several times with a flashlight since the electricity was not yet turned on. They found nothing. They were not disturbed after that or else they became accustomed to strange noises.

After the State took over, one of the architects admitted thinking she had overslept one morning when it was her turn to cook breakfast. Hurriedly she went downstairs, got things going, and was having a quick cup of coffee while waiting for the rest of the crew.

She was astonished when a quick glance at her watch revealed that it was not yet five o'clock. She had heard footsteps in the hall and had supposed it was part of her group. Later she found they had all slept soundly!

During the several years when the house had stood vacant, shepherds in the area refused to take shelter in the Mansion, even during storms. They complained of music, laughter, and voices coming from the ballroom and footsteps around different rooms of the house were too ghostly to be endured.

One state employee confessed to me that he enjoyed working at the Dorsey Mansion but always left before dark.

So far as is known, the basement workman is the only violent death to occur at this site, so maybe he persuades the music to play and the dancers to dance!

No one has reported any ghostly manifestations at Point of Rocks, about a mile away, where a stagecoach and guards were set upon by a roving band of renegade Indians. Eleven persons were slain and left sprawled among the rock.

Meanwhile, Dorsey, who wanted to be a cattle baron, began buying stock from local ranchers. He was prone to be arrogant in dealing with them and was said to chisel them out of even a thin dime, if he could. This did not make him a popular figure with the local people.

He had the habit of sitting astride a blooded Arabian stallion at a nearby small hill below the house, where he could count the cattle purchased as they were herded past him.

A yellow steer was usually the herd leader and Stephen never knew that the steer led the herds around the point of the hill, over the hill, and through a sort of sway-back area, and right past him again. He was paying for the same cows, sometimes as much as three times! Had he treated the local ranchers like human beings they would have helped him in any way.

During roundups, even today, a cowboy new to the region sometimes reports he was unable to lay a rope on a peculiar "yellow" critter, nor could he track him.

Around this hill point is the Ingersoll place, now owned by

the Seward family of Alaska purchase fame. This place was built by Dorsey as a gift to the famed atheist lawyer, Robert Ingersoll, who defended Dorsey during the star mail route scandals.

Dorsey, using his Washington influence, had secured several star mail routes in this sparsely settled area, and was supposed to be delivering mail on schedules varying from three times weekly to once weekly. It was soon found that the routes were being serviced haphazardly with some only once a month or so.

Ingersoll managed to secure Dorsey's acquittal on mail fraud charges, but this was the beginning of the end for this ambitious man. He had incurred sizeable debts, made bad deals with large sums of money, and lost out with his lifelong ability to charm money from richer contacts.

Eventually he had to give up his Mansion and took Helen to Colorado where he tried his hand at mining ventures but again was unsuccessful. He finally left for the west coast and it was out there that he died, an impoverished man.

Restoration of the Dorsey Mansion is quite an expensive job. The State has begun where the Deatons left off, but it is not yet completed so that visitors must wait for an announcement as to when they may wander through the old place again.

Dorsey wasn't successful in New Mexico but he did leave his mark on the state. There is, of course, the unbelievable Mansion, used for many things since his day! Then there are the ruins of Chico that grew up to house workmen and servants. The city of Clayton, New Mexico, was named for his son, Clayton. A statue of Kit Carson in Santa Fe was erected by him. Then there are hosts of tales of great affairs when the beautiful Helen presided as hostess at a proud Mansion on the prairie.

FORT UNION

New Mexico Territory, in 1821-46, belonged to Mexico. The U.S. was growing a bump on the head they called Manifest Destiny, and that called for taking the Mexican Territory of New Mexico (which then embraced Arizona, and southern Calfornia) and making it a part of the United States.

Stephen Watts Kearny led a group of U.S. soldiers over Raton pass and down the old "Trace" (Santa Fe Trail) — taking possession of the country as they moved south. Kearny received a field commission as General as the conquering army moved successfully, finally into the Territorial Capitol of Santa Fe on August 18, 1846, where he raised the U.S. flag over El Palacio — the Palace of the Governors. The Mexicans were poorly organized, and their government incohesive. Kearny took the Capitol without firing a shot. One yarn has it that Armijo, the Mexican governor, fleeing south, carried a bag of coins and when pursuers got too close, he threw out a couple of handfuls. The pursuers, it was said, stopped and searched until they were sure they had found them all before mounting their steeds and riding after the errant governor again. The whole yarn sounds a bit rhetorical but it is a good yarn, true or false.

Back in Santa Fe, Kearny promptly ordered Army Engineers to select a site and draw up plans for a fort to be a center for the holding of this new land. They chose a hilltop overlooking the city of Santa Fe and promptly began the building of Fort Marcy.

The Fort itself progressed very rapidly, while officer's quarters, stables, barracks, a hospital, and other necessary adjuncts sprawled downhill onto the Plaza — which occupied seventeen acres of the downtown area.

Having gotten a functioning government funding, Kearny, who had an itchy foot and a big ambition, started west to take California.

The soldiers liked Santa Fe and had a royal good time, even to building a gazebo in the Plaza for concerts, a swank parade ground over on what is today Federal Place, and the town itself provided plenty of amusement. *Fandangos* (dances), gambling, drinking, all were common. Wine and Taos Lightning — a very potent raw whiskey, were readily available.

In 1851 the War Department sent Col. E. V. Sumner to command the forces in Santa Fe. Poor Col. Sumner was shocked from head to toe by Santa Fe. Santa Fe women were not only pretty, they wore dresses with off-shoulder blouses, and had no qualms about showing their shapely ankles. They rolled their own cigarettes with corn husks, danced with verve and style, played faro and other gambling games with Fort Marcy soldiers subsidizing them; the local Hispanic men were a bit less than happy.

Col. Sumner promptly discarded the Territorial Fort and moved the major portion of Fort Marcy to a location north of Las Vegas, then known as Holes in the Prairie.

Here he built the first of three forts that ultimately became known as Fort Union. There are still a few walls from this Fort, close to the foothills — and close to a rapidly growing village called Loma Parda — just over the hump of hills. Loma Parda was inhabited by not only farmers, but rustlers of the plains who specialized in raiding cattle herds, stealing herds, horses, supplies from the wagon trains crossing from Independence, Kansas, to New Mexico.

No sooner was the first Fort Union established than officers noted that the men had seemingly developed a passion for rockhounding on the close-by hills. A little snooping proved that the large population of "soiled doves" at Loma Parda had cribs in

Ruins of Fort Union, New Mexico, ca 1940. Photo courtesy Museum of New Mexico (Neg. No. 1825).

among the rocks and were doing a thriving business.

In addition, a crude road was cut over the hill to Loma Parda where saloons, gambling, prostitution were added to the early cattle and horse thievery and a fair amount of highjacking, assault on the soldiers, sometimes murder became ordinary. Putting Loma Parda, sometimes called Sodom on the Mora because the village straddled the tiny Mora River, off limits for Fort personnel simply could not be enforced. Military Police simply joined the soldiers until they were all broke or tired out. Men "lost" their side arms consistently, and military issued pistols were routinely found on the Comancheros, as the organized bands of thieves were soon branded. Poor Col. Sumner! Trying to get the Army out of the baleful influence of Santa Fe only to dump them into a much more sinful environment. Army officials were never able to control Loma Parda, or keep soldiers out of the place.

Meanwhile another Fort was built further away from the foothills, only to give way to the final Fort Union, sometimes called the Star Fort, due to the star shape of the outer walls, still discernible by air as low ridges.

With all the killing during robberies, fights over gambling games, it seems strange that the ghosts at Fort Union do not turn to these violent deaths. Instead, the final Fort was well built, with parade grounds, officers' homes, mess halls, a hospital jail, recreation hall, and shooting ranges.

Soldiers told of seeing parties, dances, etc., going on in the recreation building after it was torn down. It frightened them and they quickly made their way back to the barracks, and usually didn't mention it until something got one of the men to talking, which led others to confess to the same experience. Reports of the ghostly parties are rare today, but reports of Gen. U.S. Grant continue to surface fairly often.

Reports were uniformly casual — a caretaker, visitor, whatever, asks about the tall man in the Civil War period uniform who walks from the parade ground to the hospital, walks through the door space, and simply cannot be located when followed. There doesn't seem to be a particular time of day — or night — for this completely solid looking apparition.

The Union Land Grant and Grazing Company had charge of the Fort Union acreage for some time after the Fort was closed, as it was no longer necessary to protect travelers and act as a supply depot for other forts in the state. Capt. E.B. Wheeler was agent in charge for the Cattle Company. He had earned his Captain's bars at the Fort before it closed.

Wheeler loved the old Fort site and protected the ruins as best he could. His officers were in the upstairs portion of People's Saving Bank in Las Vegas but he kept men patrolling the Fort Union acreage. His men had told him about the heavily bearded man walking to the old hospital but he dismissed the story as inconsequential until he saw him himself. "It can't be, of course, but it was General (later President) Grant so I just don't talk about it. People would say I was getting senile," he told me.

Now Fort Union is a National Monument, with a nice headquarters building that is offices and a Museum, people who protect and care for the ruins of Fort buildings. It's well worth the visit, and is located on a turnoff just north of Watrous, New Mexico, which is fun, *too*. The whole village is a National Landmark.

Lt. Gen. U.S. Grant. Photo courtesy Museum of New Mexico (Neg. No. 89471).

TSANKAWI

Tsankawi is an inconspicuous little mesa top within the Bandelier National Park. Finding it isn't difficult if you begin to watch the lefthand side of the highway to Bandelier shortly before White Rock. There is a sign for Tsankawi but it isn't the flamboyant cocktail lounge type. Instead, it is a small innocuous sign marking a footpath. It is necessary to park carefully on the highway.

The circular footpath meanders among the scrub oak growing thickly down to a narrow gate. There is an office, as yet unmanned, and a box on a fence post where one may pick up a pamphlet. You may keep this if you care to pay a coin or so or you may return it when you leave.

The path is marked, as National Parks do, but Tsankawi has had no excavation done as yet. Personally, I hope they don't for Tsankawi has such a primitive and native appeal. I don't want it "cleaned up."

A platform of sheet rock emerges after a short climb, and so controlled is it in appearance, one thinks the primitive Indians of the mesa had laid it as a dance platform, until you look closely. The platform is all in one large sheet of rock without cracks or seams of any kind. From this area the Park Service path climbs gently and trails through ancient tufa beds. Here bare-feet or sandals have worn several paths ankle deep into the rock. It's unbelievable, but there it is!

Winding through piled up rock formations, the paths widen on top of the thumb-shaped mesa that sticks out into the wide valley on three sides. The pueblos that once stood here are easily discernible although centuries of rain, snow and wind have taken their toll. The soft mounds are covered with scattered wild flowers. Primrose, loco weed, paint brush, sheep shower, etc., blanket the area. They grow taller in the patio area where several kiva circles conserve the sparse rainfall and give it to the growing plants. There are a few shards of long ago shattered pottery.

Please leave them there. Even if you only take one small piece it would soon be gone and that tiny piece would lose its identity in a drawer with no one remembering where it came from after a time.

The pinon jays, swallows, a robin or so, flit around and once in awhile a cottontail or jackrabbit lopes off into the bush.

The footpath leads ahead to the edge of the cliff that wraps around the mesa edges. The Park Service has constructed a pueblo type ladder, sturdy and solid to descend to the lower path and back to the entrance gate. The cliff has a few discernible cave houses painfully gouged out of the rock and a half-dozen or so viga holes where once a pueblo type nestled tight up against the stone.

Interesting petroglyphs are found on the rocks just before arriving at the pueblo site on the mesa, and again here.

The lower path climbs and descends erratically around the base of the cliff, but it is easy walking. I could find no place where it looked as though the Tsankawi got any water, even for household use. There must have been a spring about somewhere.

Cavate Ruins, Tsankawi, Bandelier National Monument, New Mexico
Photo by E.W. Northnagel, courtesy Museum of New Mexico
(Neg. No. 59339)

Tsankawi isn't too well-known and hence there aren't many visitors, even from the surrounding area. The quiet is intense until a little imagination is needed to feel the pinon trees stretching down the slope toward the valley tell each other secrets and mayhap have their opinion of those loud-voiced human beings that tramp through with clumsy feet or sit in our shade and eat sandwiches while tossing bits of bread crust to the ground squirrels who sit and seemingly beg as they chirrup to each other.

The valley is relatively smooth and excellent for cattle grazing since there are very few bushes or trees marking the fields of gramma grass. It is in this valley that we have our ghosts for Tsankawi.

The first report I had of them came from an Oklahoma honeymoon couple who came to ask if there had been a ranch there at one time. This pair having met the winter before at the Hyde Park ski run had fallen in love, married, and came back to the area for their June honeymoon.

I knew of no ranch on this side of the mesa and investigation found no one else who knew of such an establishment. The young couple told of looking down into the valley in mid-afternoon and seeing what seemed to be a dance party of six or eight people in an old patio.

There was no sound even though they could see a fiddler and a guitarist seated on kitchen chairs atop a long table. This custom was prevalent in this area in the old days. The musicians could watch the dancers and they, in turn, could see the players.

The scene was so clear they were able to see that the dancing guests seemed to be doing so on their knees. As they watched, it dawned on them finally, that the patio floor must have been filled with dirt, weeds, and other debris so that the ghostly party was dancing on the original floor. They had, they said, the impression of a small adobe house back of the patio but weren't sure. Their eyes were on the dancers and the musicians on the table.

I have inquired, widely, for others who may have seen this patio and its activity or anything that resembled it. Only one, a male hiker, had seen a small group of very short people in old-type Spanish costumes and in the same location but they weren't dancing.

Maybe the "spirits" were dancing to honor the young novios from a neighboring state. Wedding dances were, and still are, very popular among native peoples.

CORONADO STATE MONUMENT

When Coronado and his men spent the winter of 1540 in New Mexico, it is known that he took possession of one of a group of pueblos along the Rio Grande. Whether this was by invitation or force is not clear. Nor is it absolutely provable just which of the pueblos he took for shelter, but evidence strongly points to the one that is today known as the Coronado Monument.

A great deal of restoration and exploratory work has been done here, and the State Park Service has a small but very nice headquarters building, well cared for walls, benches here and there for visitors to rest weary bones, and a small but very friendly crew to direct, aid visitors, and answer questions. Some of this crew is, of course, highly trained, but there are also workers for maintenance from the surrounding area.

One of these maintenance workers was, so the story goes, a fine young lad from Jemez Pueblo, just north among the majestic slopes of the Jemez mountains. Gossip had it that the Jemez lad was the grandson of a Jemez Pueblo Shaman. Certainly the lad was a dependable worker, quiet, polite, with deep, brooding eyes.

One day, in early spring, the lad asked if he could come to work at daylight the next day and leave early. The boy said he wanted to go see his "Abuelo" (grandfather) who had been ill and was getting no better.

"Go ahead, lad," the supervisor said. "Take what time you need and come back when you can."

The supervisor was sitting on the stile steps over an ancient adobe wall the next morning, tying his shoelace, when the Jemez boy came across the Plaza of the great restored Kiva. The supervisor, planning on a fishing trip, was in no hurry. He was genuinely fond of the boy, and wondered if the gossip he had heard was true. He had been told the lad was studying the ancient art of Shamanism under his grandfather.

Kuaua Pueblo Ruins (Coronado State Monument) near Bernalillo, New Mexico, ca 1940. Photo courtesy Museum of New Mexico.

It was a cloudy, gray day with the Sandia mountains, across the river, looking cold and purple in the pre-sunrise light. Just as the Jemez boy came abreast of the poles of the Kiva ladder, seemingly out of nowhere a great horned owl sailed in and perched on the top crossbar of the ladder. The bird seemed to be looking straight at the Indian lad. The boy paused, raised his right arm with palm outward, then slowly lowered it. He walked slowly around the Kiva with the almost shuffling tread of the women's dance, his eyes on the owl. The owl did not move a muscle except his neck. It twisted smoothly so that his gaze never left the shuffling figure. The boy finally stopped, facing the East, crossed his arms over his chest, and softly chanted what seemed to be a prayer. He then turned and trotted swiflty across the field in the direction of his home Pueblo. The supervisor rose, dusted off his pants, and looked at the Kiva ladder. The owl was no longer there though he had heard no movement of wings.

The supervisor somehow lost all desire to fish and walked back to headquarters. He felt very strange, lonely and sad for no reason.

The Jemez boy never came back, though one of the Jemez workers told the supervisor one of the wise men at the pueblo had died — the Shaman known as Great Owl. He was asked about the boy, but shrugged and said he didn't know where he was.

The supervisor remembered the straight young figure of the boy, facing the East, palm held high, and decided he didn't really need to know.

QUARAI

Three of the so-called Saline Pueblos located southeast of the Manzano mountains in central New Mexico have magnificent mission church ruins.

Gran Quivira was the first to become a National Monument but now all three, Gran Quivira, Quarai and Abo are under the federal government. Quarai had been owned by the State of New Mexico since 1913, when three men in Mountainair donated the site to the state. It had been administered by the Museum of New Mexico as Quarai State Monument. And so had been Abo. They are now known as Salinas National Monument.

The Coronado Expedition came to New Mexico in 1540. Their first pueblo visit was what is now Zuni. Then they moved over to the valley of the Rio Grande, but the first Spaniards to enter the Salinas area came with the little expedition led by Captain Francisco Chamuscado and Fray Augustin Rodriguez. These men discovered five pueblos during the winter of 1581-1583, but spent very little time among them. Permanent Spanish settlement of New Mexico dates from 1598. In October of that year Governor Don Juan de Onate spent ten days touring the Salinas pueblos.

The Indian people there were agricultural in emphasis rather than the roving, more war-like Apache, Navajo, or Comanche tribes. They were wary of strangers, for, being as they were on the edge of the buffalo plains, they were far too often raided for food, their flocks of turkeys, grain storage, pelts and weaving. Often their women and children were taken as slaves.

The Spaniards were so far advanced in their technology the Indians weren't sure whether they were human or some species of strange new gods.

The first horsemen frightened them badly. A strange new beast with great teeth that could split itself up and then get back together. They had never seen a horse nor horseman dismounting and then mounting again. And what looked like men were so different. They had hair on their faces, carried sticks that spoke with the voice of thunder and spat death like unto lightning. The flying death spit out by these strange sticks pierced the Indian shells and dealt death quickly and easily.

The breasts and heads of these strangers shone in the sun. Indian arrows clashed with a dull sound and dropped harmlessly to the ground. The invaders walked over the sacred cornmenal trails on Mother Earth as though they were dust.

Under the power exhibited by the Spanish, the Indian population succumbed rapidly. It wasn't that they were not brave, for they were, but they were also sensible.

The Spanish conquerors themselves were divided — those who believed in the military and those who were for the church. There was a great deal of competition and the Indians were caught in the middle. The military demanded the Indians unpaid service as servants, hunters, farmers, and menial jobs of all kinds.

The churchmen, in their capacity as savers of Indian souls, also demanded menial services, growing food, furnishing wood, and a huge amount of time spent on erecting churches and conventos. The Friars had architectural skills of a high degree, for the churches in this area were of a size sufficient to serve any city in New Mexico today.

The earliest mention of Quarai occurs in a 1628 reference to Fray Juan Gutierrez de la Chica as resident priest at the convento.

Quarai Mission Ruins, Salinas National Monument, New Mexico, ca 1940. Photo by De Castro, courtesy Museum of New Mexico (Neg. No. 58328).

But it may have been Fray Juan, another priest who came in 1633, or someone else, who actually supervised the building of La Purisima Concepcion. Built by the Indians of Quarai, without benefit of European tools of any kind, under the supervision of their architect-friar, it is cruciform in plan. Sandstone walls that originally stood some 40 feet high, while the interior was 100 feet in length and the maximum width of the transept is 50 feet. The walls that remain standing are awe-inspiring even today.

The most intriguing story is not about a ghost but that of "The Blue Lady." It may be called a religious epic, a miracle, or whatever you choose, but it remains fascinating. Even today there are those that are researching and seeking to document.

When Fray Alonso Benavides, who was custodio of all the missions in New Mexico territory, began hearing repeated requests for more padres for Quarai, in particular from the Indians who asked for more priestly services and particularly baptism. On being questioned as to why, they answered that "The Blue Lady" had instructed them to demand and "be not slothful about it," baptism and the hole rites of Christianity.

They spoke of a beautiful Lady in Blue who would walk into their plaza and talk with them in their own language. She told them of God, Jesus, and Joseph and Mary. She healed the sick including the son of the chief who lay dying. She bathed his fevered brow, talked to him, giving him low-voiced commands then demanded gruel and fresh water.

Another story was that of a young wife who had been in labor far too long. The Blue Lady ordered her to stretch out on a buffalo robe and relax her muscles as much as she could. The baby must be reversed, she told the attending women. Her hips were too narrow to allow a breech birth.

With strong, but delicate hands, the Lady massaged and turned the child, still in the mother's body, until the position was changed. Within a half hour the baby was born. The exhausted mother fell asleep as the midwives cared for the infant.

When a visit from the Lady came and there was no illness to be treated, the Indians gathered around and she talked again to them about the strange God, Jesus, who was dead on a wooden cross, and his family — Joseph and Mary. They really couldn't understand why, if he had been buried and came back alive, the Lady still carried the cross with the dead figure on it. Keeping the dead was bad, it allowed the spirit to ride the night winds, perhaps taking the breath of a living person, leaving him lifeless on the trail.

The Indians also thought it strange that the Lady always spoke to them in their own language but never spoke to a Spanish friar nor a soldier. They didn't seem to see her but indeed, walked right by as though she were not there. The Lady instructed them often to demand priests and baptism of the Spanish. They did as she told them, only to meet with bewildered shakes of the head and perhaps a doubtful question or so.

As the years rolled on, life became more difficult for the Salinas Indians and the area. Padres were sent sparingly and for that they could not but feel thankful. The military demanded the services of the male Indians for duties of all kinds and without any compensation, of course.

When the padres came, they began the building of the missions and demanded more and more of them, men and women, to do the construction as well as the maintenance of their households. They needed food, wood to keep warm, and water to be carried for daily use.

Demands on the Indians increased at the building of the great flagstone churches at Gran Quivira, Quarai and Abo. Even the Indians stood in awe at the height of the walls and the great dimensions. The Indians were drafted into chipping, without tools of any kind, except what they, themselves, had evolved and the Padres had learned.

There were too few to work the fields and grow food. Raids by the roving bands of Apache, Comanche, Kiowa, and even the Navajo increased as a season of drought, all too frequent on these plains, set in.

The death rate among the Indians rose. Undernourished bodies did not, could not, fight the new diseases that came with the conquerors. Measles, with the Hispanics, were soon overcome, but not with the Indians who had no immunity to this strange splotching of their skin, the high fever, and too often death. So, too, with smallpox, the cough that tore life-blood from the lungs, and other ailments they had no names for.

Men and women died of the punishments meted out to them for failure to meet the work-load assigned to their undernourished bodies. Babies born of frail women often failed to utter the first wail of protest at their entry into this cruel world.

Fray Benavides listened to the Indians but more carefully than others had done, and in particular, to the stories about the Blue Lady. A fellow friar at Socorro had a small hand-painted medallion of his blood sister, now a sister in a Spanish order of women who wore the blue habit described by the Indians.

Fray Benavides showed them the portrait and asked if this was their Blue Lady. They shook their heads negatively, telling him the dress was the same but that the face — their lady was far more beautiful. Fray Benavides also listened carefully to the stories of the men who accompanied Onate to the southwest and the gulf of California. They had seen the Blue Lady and told of shooting arrows that went right through her. She noticed them but the musket fire was just as ineffective. Just as at Quarai, she walked in, spoke to the people in their own tongue, never tasted food or water, and walked out again. Her visits were never longer than a couple of hours.

It is extremely doubtful if Friar Benavides heard any stories of the Blue Lady from other places, other than from the people of New Mexico. News was extremely slow in travel in the days of no telephone, radio, television or fast travel. But what he heard in the area entrusted to him intrigued him tremedously.

When he traveled back to Spain, he was determined to investigate the Blue Lady at the headquarters of the Franciscan order at Agreda in the province of Soria. There he talked to Maria de Jesus, now Mother Superior at the convent, and was astonished at the things he was told. The Mother Superior had been born at Agreda and had never physically left Spain, joining the religious order when she was but 17. To make it a family affair, her mother also entered the convent and her father and another brother became Franciscans.

Mother Superior freely told Benavides that when she entered her sleeping cell and dropped off to sleep on the hard plank bed, she traveled in spirit to this new contry. She told him things she could not have learned in any normal way about Quarai and details of church affairs that Benavides knew to be correct for he had presided at them.

Spanish people never seemed to see her, she said, but the Indians all could. The nun freely admitted that in these flights, which occurred at any time of the day or night, that when alone, she closed her eyes, and spoke the tongue of any people that she visited, but only so long as she was with them.

When the church authorities were informed of Mother Superior's adventures, they promptly forbade any more flights, but stories continued to be told of her appearances in Texas, New Mexico, Arizona, and southern California.

The Blue Lady's tiny cell at the convent in Agreda is still preserved today, as well as the chains she wore around her waist, the painful garments she wore under her habit, her crucifix, and original copies of the manuscripts of two books she wrote.

Back in this country, the three major pueblos of the Salinas group probably carried the seeds of their own destruction, for New Mexico is subject to recurring droughts. With the demands on manpower made by the church and the military, the raids of roving tribes, and the death rate from disease, the whole area was deserted before the Pueblo Rebellion of 1680. The remnants of the people made homes with friendly tribes along the Rio Grande, including Isleta and the pueblos in what is today, the Bernalillo area.

The Salinas became known locally as the "Cities that died of fear," for the raids of nomadic tribes were often blamed for the deaths of these pueblos without any mention of other causes.

Today, the ruins of the great missions at Gran Quivira, Quarai, and Abo are often compared by world travelers to the ruins of castles along the Rhine.

Stories often surface at group picnics or suppers at the ruins of Quarai. It was a popular spot for lodge, church, scout, or other gatherings, and for those who lingered late on nights of the full moon, came stories of hearing the music of the pipe organ and Indian choirs lasting several minutes at the "witching hour" of midnight.

A newspaper report in the late 1890's tells of a party of hunters camped in the nave of the old church, and who were waked by noise of clanking arms, voices raised in anger, terror, or in a combination of both. They saw Indians being chased through the walls still standing by soldiers in full Spanish armor of the 1600's. They disappeared as they paid no attention to the mission walls, hurrying through as though they had never existed.

Old-time residents will sometimes tell, on being assured their names will not be printed, of either hearing Indian drums or seeing a naked Indian runner hurrying to a pueblo site. If they didn't experience this themselves, it was a member of their family before the area was exposed to automobile lights, trucks, or other noisy implements of modern travel.

"The railroad scared a lot of them away," one toothless old-timer said. "We used to man the torreons at night so we wouldn't be caught by anybody sneaking up on us — real or ghost!"

LINCOLN TOWN

Anyone who loves ghost stories and deliberately hunts them, sometimes gets excited about one, hunts to find the sources, and ends up with disappointment. All ghost yarns are not authentic of course. Neither are news releases, or for that matter "historical" records.

I was real excited about a Lincoln County yarn when I first heard it. Lincoln County is historically significant and highly interesting. It was the center of the events tht led to the Lincoln County War in southern New Mexico. The Murphy and Dolan gang, offshoots of the notorious Santa Fe Ring, got in there a bit early, established business connections that were highly lucrative, and naturally wanted to hang onto their assets. A retail store did a land office business, even loaned ranchers money — with high interest rates, naturally. Cattle business was lucrative and anyone who didn't like the gang's methods could go lump it. The gang controlled the Territorial law forces, and certainly didn't welcome the Englishman, John Henry Tunstall, a man the natives were prone to call an "innocente." It wasn't that he wasn't a nice man. He was. But he just was not smart about local practices. He was, indeed, a bit foolish, which is the local translation for "innocente."

John Henry Tunstall was from a wealthy English family, determined to make a fortune by cattle ranching and merchandising in this new and fascinating country. He put in a general store and charged reasonable prices in addition to his ranching business. To say that the Dolan-Murphy gang resented this was putting it mildly, naturally. They were losing too much money to the English dude.

The inevitable happened when the Englishman was shot in the back while riding cross-country with a few of his hands.

John Henry Tunstall had become an almost fatherly figure to William Bonney, alias Billy the Kid, by giving him a job and treating him decently. Billy swore to kill every man who had had a part in this murder, and his trigger finger went to work. He meant it and the really bloody beginning of the Lincoln County War got under way in earnest. It also put legal authorities on the trail of the Kid, who gave the established gang a "tit-for-tat" existence. Undoubtedly he not only participated in free-wheeling shoot-outs but in cattle rustling and horse stealing as well.

Billy was popular in the community and many folks felt that he only did what most of the young folks embroiled in this cattle and merchandising war did as a matter of course — for survival. Billy, however, had a certain flair and a fairly waggish tongue. When the "war" was pretty well over, he continued to gamble, dance, and rustle cattle as usual.

Rewards went out for his capture, and eventually he was killed at the home of an old friend by newly-elected Sheriff Pat Garrett. He had little other than local reputation until Walter Burns Noble, a writer, made him a hero in his book about him in 1925.

Billy had been jailed several times on various charges, and on one occasion had shot his way out of the Lincoln County Courthouse jail in Lincoln.

The old Courthouse-jail still stands in Lincoln, and stories about it and its most famous prisoner proliferated. One of these

Lincoln County Courthouse, Lincoln, New Mexico. Photo courtesy Museum of New Mexico (Neg. No. 11634).

stories had to do with the recreation room in the Courthouse. Billiards was a very popular game and the Courthouse sported a billiard table.

Incarceration in the Licnoln County War period was vastly different from today's standards. A prisoner was lucky to be allowed a deck of cards, which he furnished, or a checker board and checkers to play with a fellow inmate. *Nothing* was furnished, so it goes without saying that chained-up Billy the Kid was not taken downstairs to play billairds or pool with the Sheriff at the Courthouse, but when the racked-up balls on the table were found morning after morning knocked all over the table, and sometimes one or two on the floor, word spread. "Billy the Kid's ghost is playing pool at the Courthouse."

Windows were checked — all secure and locked. The door was locked and the key carried to the Courthouse safe for guarantee purposes. Still the balls on the table continued to be in disarray morning after morning. Examination of the room by deputies when balls were heard clinking revealed nothing — no one there. It had to be a ghost.

One deputy, a case-hardened officer of long standing, asked for permission to sleep under the table and see what he could learn.

Alas! The ghost disappeared with the yellow tail of a skinny alley cat, who evidently like playing with pool balls. He was squeezing through a slit in the bottom of a bookcase built into the wall adjacent to another room. Officials disposed of the cat — and the ghost — in one operation!

CITY OF ROCKS

New Mexico and Arizona were originally one state under the name New Mexico. It was, of course, much too large to be effectively governed, particularly before the days of railroads, highways, and even decent wagon roads. Eventually the area was split with a north-south division line to the present two states — New Mexico and Arizona.

Many think the division, while necessary, should have been made with the division line running east-west because of the character of the terrain. Most of the northern half of both states is mountainous while the southern half runs to gently sloping foothills, grasslands, finally leveling out into the desert country of northern Mexico. There are areas of timber in the southern half, of course, but they do not predominate.

Among the miles of prairie land, good cattle country, around Silver City and Deming, there is a *vast* area of rolling hills that is unique in that the ridge of one long chain is dominated by roughly stacked stone cliffs and protrusions in such a manner that the motorist driving in feels he is seeing the tall buildings of a metropolis skylined against perfect blue skies. There are no trees or shrubs (other than the tall yucca elata) growing in the area which emphasizes the feel of what it has been so aptly named "City of Rocks." The State of New Mexico has marked this area as a State Monument area, put in roads and foot trails, and the City of Rocks has become quite popular.

The ghost story here is not a pretty one, caused by an all-too-frequent occurrence in modern times. An independent young lady (in her early twenties) spread out her sleeping bag and tiny camp spirit stove before the state took over. It was a beautiful spot with ripples of brown gramma grass rippling in the slightest breeze, and as dark cloaked the bulk of the stone monoliths the lonesome howl of a coyote calling his mate was heard now and then. She felt perfectly safe as she dropped of to sleep.

It was not a nightmare that woke her, but two young men,

pretty thoroughly liquored up, who had decided to spend the night among the rocks in their stolen pickup. They stumbled on the girl quite by accident, and she was pretty. The inevitable happened. They raped her, and then aghast at what they had done wanted no one alive to tell the lawmen, already hunting them, of their crime here as well. They strangled her and drove off to make their way into Mexico to hide out.

The girl marked the area with her personal matrix of terror. Many people camp in the area and nothing bothers them — but if two men, with no female companions, drive into the area at night they find their own terror. Their car or pickup is suddenly enveloped in an impenetrable cloak of dark, not a flicker of light — no stars, no moon, no lone campfire, not even their cigarette lighters will produce even the muted flare of a single candle in the dark sack surrounding them.

Their motor will run, but their headlights are dead — even the dashboard is a blank, black area of mystery. There are no sounds. No bodily touches from the cul-de-sac in which they find themselves. They don't need anything to augment the terror that grips them — complete blindness. Their car will run, but when that is done they can see no roads, or even the gigantic boulders. They run into one, or off the gently slope into a minor arroyo bed, the bumping and wobbling of the vehicle augmenting their fear. If they don't wreck their vehicle they finally sit numbly, shivering, and too frightened to even talk.

When morning comes the sun lightens the shadows, the black hole in which they had been encased melts away. They don't as a rule, talk about their adventure for who would believe them?

Even with a wrecked car the tow truck driver grins and admonishes them to watch out about tequila — the Mexican popular liquor from south of the border, and hitches up their stalled vehicle for the haul into town, whistling cheerfully.

WHITE SANDS

The southern part of New Mexico has a great deal of starkly beautiful, rather arid, acreage. The Valley of the Tularosa is included in this area. Great dunes of sparkling white gypsum gleam in the shadows of the San Andres Mountains, so rugged in outline, that they look more like painted stage backdrops than natural formation.

There is an old Indian legend that gives a feel of unreal reality to the Tularosa. According to this legend, the Tularosa Valley was once pretty fair farm land and near where the White Sands Monument Visitor's Center now stands, there was a relatively small Indian pueblo.

The people in the Pueblo were a peace-loving, kindly people having no trouble with any of the other tribes then scattered through what is New Mexico or sprawling down to the Sonora desert area of Sonora.

They were a strongly religious group, worshipping the Sun Father, Earth Mother, and the many manifestations of nature as well as life in all its forms.

One night one of their Shamans, an ancient, wise and prophetic personality, had a dream or a vision, if you will. In this vision he saw a great canoe, much larger than any ever seen by people of the area. It had white wings that did not flap in the breeze but were, instead, filled and rounded by the winds. It was headed for this continent with men who were exceedingly strange. Their faces had hair that hung down over their chests and they wore dazzling white blankets that looked hard, solid, and clanked when they walked. They carried with them strange beasts, larger than deer or antelope, but none were horned and their backs were broad.

In the vision the Shaman knew, without knowing how he knew, that these strangers were warlike and that the Indians could not successfully fight them.

Shaman awoke, shaking uncontrollably on his buffalo skin

White Sands National Monument near Alamogordo, New Mexico. Photo courtesy Museum of New Mexico (Neg. No. 56446).

that adorned his sleeping blanket. The sky was dull gray as though Father Sun was angry with his children. He covered his face. The peaks of the mountains were sharp and forbidding against the skyline.

Quickly, the Shaman arose and called aloud to the sleeping people to come to the plaza at once. They had never heard such urgency in the voice of their beloved advisor. As they crowded around him, the old ones shook bewildered heads and were unable to interpret the meaning of the vision. But they were afraid and even the small children did not clamor for their morning rations of amole — a mixture of cornmeal and water, sometimes sweetened with honey when a beehive had been raided by a hunting party.

The turkeys gobbled in their pens protesting not being herded to the field to find their own food. Even the dogs were restless and whined.

A decision was made, finally, to send one young hunter and one maiden to the sacred altar high on the side of the San Andres mountains. The most potent of their magic was used in making the prayer plumes they were to carry. Their dancing of prayers on the plaza was exquisitely modulated.

Thus, it was one day later that the hunter and maiden virtually crawled, with down-cast eyes and heavy hearts, to the altar where they planted the prayer plumes after sweeping the area with sacred plumes of cedar.

The answer came as the young people sat before the altar with crossed legs and bowed heads. They were thinking of the strangers, with hairy faces, that were called Spaniards. Nothing could stop them from coming. They carried with them slender sticks that spoke with the voice of thunder and killed as did the lightning. The strange animals were horses and mules. The Spaniards rode on their backs and had them carry camping gear, extra food, and water. On them they would sweep across the land, leaving death and a new way of life that was not in keeping with the Indian ways.

They carried illnesses that would kill the Indian, sparing neither the young nor the old.

"What can we do?" asked the pair. "Is there no way for us?"

"You have been good people," the soft, sighing wind in the trees told them. "Go back to the pueblo. Gather all the people and tell them that they are to sleep inside the pueblo tonight — not on the roof nor in the fields. Put the turkeys in their pens and cover the ceremonial eagles with mantas. Tie the dogs securely. Cover all the fires until not a spark is left. No one is to look out the doors or leave his sleeping blanket for any reason.

"We, your gods, cannot keep the strangers away. All we can do is save you until they are gone. That will be a long, long time, but you will sleep happily and it will seem but a night to you."

The young couple went back to the Pueblo and the people did as they had been told.

As a new moon rose over the sleeping Pueblo, a soft mist of glistening crystals began to fall, evenly, slowly, gently, until it covered the fields, the animal pens, the Pueblo, the upper valley along the tiny river that split the Valley of the Tularosa. Gradually, all familiar landmarks were covered and the snow-like substance did not melt but stirred restlessly in the changeable breezes.

White men with hairy faces, hard suits, and shoes, and roving eyes, saw not the fields and Pueblo building, but only gleaming mounds of gypsum, so they rode past.

The Indians sleep on and when the invader is gone the gypsum will roll back and they will herd the turkeys back to the fields, plant their corn, melons, squash, teach their children to revere life in the old way and all will be as before.

THE BRIDAL COUPLE

A sad, but perhaps real, ghost story is told of the White Sands and an early-day school teacher from Alamogordo.

She, and her fiance, who was from another city, were to be married the day after school was out for the summer. He came in on the last day of school and since the wedding was to be a very quiet one at the home of the minister, the teacher prepared a picnic supper and took him out to the White Sands. He had never seen the area and was fascinated by the shifting dunes.

After supper, while she packed the picnic hampers, he decided to walk to the top of the largest dune, just back of their auto. There was a moderate wind and his footsteps were covered almost as fast as he made them.

She looked up, waved, and called for him to come back as everything was packed and in the car trunk. But that was the last time she ever saw him. No one knows what happened. He was just gone without a trace though search parties hunted diligently.

Even though all hope was gone she drove out to the picnic spot, calling and hunting. Then, one day, she didn't come back either. People thought she wandered away deliberately, unable to cope with living without her lost love.

No sign of him has been reported but when the wind is fairly brisk, a number of people have thought they saw her, quite happy, and dancing along the top of a dune. Only now, she wears her wedding dress and the white sands swirl around her head, providing a finger-tip veil and the little song the sands sing is a happy one until she is out of sight.

A shy little girl told me, softly, she knows where the teacher and her man are — in the Pueblo of the old ones. They will awaken when the Indians do and the white sands roll away.

Could be!

www.ingramcontent.com/pod-product-compliance
Lightning Source LLC
Chambersburg PA
CBHW051705040426
42446CB00009B/1306